I0816524

CORE LIBRARY OF US STATES

Ohio

BY ANNA SAXTON

CONTENT CONSULTANT
Michael Mangus, PhD
Senior Lecturer of History
The Ohio State University

Core Library

An Imprint of Abdo Publishing
abdobooks.com

abdobooks.com

Published by Abdo Publishing, a division of ABDO, PO Box 398166, Minneapolis, Minnesota 55439.

Printed in the United States of America, North Mankato, Minnesota.
052022
092022

Cover Photo: Shutterstock Images
Interior Photos: Joe Hendrickson/Shutterstock Images, 4–5; Red Line Editorial, 7 (Ohio), 7 (USA); S. M. Reid/Shutterstock Images, 9; A. Provchy/Shutterstock Images, 10–11, 43; P. Harstela/Shutterstock Images, 13; Filip Bjorkman/Shutterstock Images, 15 (flag); iStockphoto, 15 (bird), 31; E. Q. Roy/Shutterstock Images, 15 (fruit); Tom Reichner/Shutterstock Images, 15 (deer); D. B. Beyer/iStockphoto, 15 (flower); William Sartain/Library of Congress, 18; Pictor Picture Company/Shutterstock Images, 20; Kenneth Keifer/Shutterstock Images, 22–23; Pat Dooley/Shutterstock Images, 25, 45; Historic American Buildings Survey/Historic American Engineering Record/Historic American Landscapes Survey/Library of Congress, 28–29; Bettmann/Getty Images, 34–35; Sean Pavone/Shutterstock Images, 38; Adam Lacy/Icon Sportswire/AP Images, 40

Editor: Marie Pearson
Series Designer: Joshua Olson

Library of Congress Control Number: 2021951565

Publisher's Cataloging-in-Publication Data

Names: Saxton, Anna, author.
Title: Ohio / by Anna Saxton
Description: Minneapolis, Minnesota : Abdo Publishing, 2023 | Series: Core library of US states | Includes online resources and index.
Identifiers: ISBN 9781532197765 (lib. bdg.) | ISBN 9781098270520 (ebook)
Subjects: LCSH: U.S. states--Juvenile literature. | Midwest States--Juvenile literature. | Ohio--History--Juvenile literature. | Physical geography--United States--Juvenile literature.
Classification: DDC 977.1--dc23

Population demographics broken down by race and ethnicity come from the 2019 census estimate. Population totals come from the 2020 census.

CONTENTS

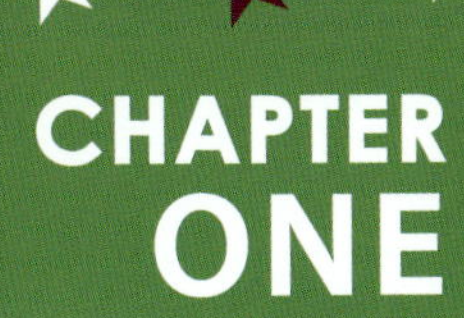

CHAPTER ONE

THE BUCKEYE STATE

Lake Erie spreads out before a group of people riding on the Millennium Force roller coaster as it climbs 310 feet (94 m) into the air. From a bird's-eye view, riders admire the blue sky and the boats skimming across the water. But the riders have only a second to appreciate the sights. Suddenly they're thrown back against their seats, zooming at 93 miles per hour (150 km/h) down the first gigantic drop. They can't help but scream.

The Cedar Point amusement park, which includes the Millennium Force roller coaster, lies on the coast of Lake Erie.

Millennium Force is just one of the 18 roller coasters at Cedar Point in Ohio. The amusement park calls itself the Roller Coaster Capital of the World. But roller coasters aren't all that Ohio's Lake Erie coastline has to offer. The area is also famous for its islands and sandy beaches. After a visit to the theme park, visitors might swim in Lake Erie's warm waters. They can fish for walleye or study the American Indian petroglyphs on Inscription Rock.

OHIO'S CENTRAL LOCATION

Ohio is famous for its central location in the United States. In fact, more than half of all households in the United States are within 600 miles (970 km) of Ohio. That means that more than half of the people in the country could drive to Ohio in just one day.

ABOUT OHIO

Ohio is part of the Midwest region of the United States. Pennsylvania is on Ohio's eastern side. West Virginia is to the southeast. Kentucky is to the south, Indiana is to the west, and Michigan is to

MAP OF OHIO

Take a close look at this map. What roles do you think bodies of water have played in Ohio's history?

Lake Erie
Toledo
Cedar Point
Cleveland
Cuyahoga Valley National Park
Cuyahoga River
Akron
Pro Football Hall of Fame
Columbus
Dayton
Hocking Hills State Park
Cincinnati
Ohio River

N
W E
S

KEY

Capital city
Park or landmark
City or town
Point of interest

PERSPECTIVES

CHURCHILL IN CINCINNATI

Winston Churchill, the prime minister of the United Kingdom, visited Cincinnati in 1932. He wrote an article for *Collier's* magazine in 1933. He said, "Cincinnati, I thought, was the most beautiful of the inland cities of the Union. From the tower of its unsurpassed hotel the city spreads far and wide its pageant of crimson, purple and gold, laced by silver streams that are great rivers."

the northwest. Because Ohio borders Lake Erie to the north, it is part of the Great Lakes region.

Historians believe that Ohio gets its name from the Haudenosaunee word *o-y-o*. This word means "great river." Ohio is also known as the Buckeye State. This nickname comes from the buckeye, a common tree in Ohio. A buckeye nut is covered in a spiky outer shell. Underneath that shell is the smooth, round nut. Some think the nut looks like the eye of a buck, or male deer. The Ohio State University adopted the buckeye as its mascot.

Ohio's state capitol building, the Ohio Statehouse, is in Columbus.

Ohio's largest cities are spread throughout the state. Columbus is in the center. It is the capital of the state and home to the Ohio State University, one of the nation's largest universities. Cincinnati is in the southwest corner, near the border with Kentucky. Cleveland is in the northeast on the shores of Lake Erie. Other large cities include Akron and Toledo. Each city has something unique to offer.

CHAPTER TWO

HISTORY OF OHIO

People have lived in Ohio since at least 9500 BCE. Archaeologists have found fossils from this time with markings from human tools. Woolly mammoths and mastodons lived in present-day Ohio when the first people arrived.

Between 1600 and 1700, modern American Indian nations began moving into Ohio. These included the Cayuga, Lenape (Delaware), Miami, Ottawa, Seneca, Shawnee, and Wyandot. Most of these peoples lived

A statue of an influential Lenape leader of the late 1700s, Konieschquanoheel, stands in Barberton.

in villages. They planted corn and other vegetables. They hunted animals including deer and bison.

EUROPEAN SETTLERS ARRIVE

In the early 1670s, the first Europeans reached Ohio. They included French, British, and Dutch fur traders and French missionaries. Fur traders were looking for beaver pelts, which were used to make fashionable hats in Europe. Though the Europeans didn't live permanently in the area, they did begin to trade with American Indians.

After the British won the French and Indian War (1756–1763), they gained control of much of the land in North America. This included present-day Ohio. They began exploring, trading, and settling. Then the United States won independence from the British in the Revolutionary War (1775–1783). After the war, Ohio's land became part of the United States. At this time, Ohio was part of the Northwest Territory.

Many beavers lived in Ohio in the 1600s.

The government encouraged Americans to move west to this territory and others.

As more people moved to present-day Ohio, fights with the American Indians broke out. The British had treated American Indians unfairly. They had charged high prices when trading. They had invaded American Indians' lands. Now American settlers wanted even more land. They wanted more space for farming and access to natural resources. After many battles, settlers forced American Indians to agree to treaties. In a 1785 treaty, the Lenape and Wyandot peoples were required to stay in the northeastern part of the region. Then in 1794 US forces defeated a group of Wyandot, Shawnee, Lenape, and Miami warriors, and their lands were restricted even further.

During the War of 1812 (1812–1815), the American Indian nations tried to regain their lands one more time. They were led by Tecumseh, a famous Shawnee warrior. After they were defeated and Tecumseh was killed in battle, they were forced to move west of what is now Ohio.

STATEHOOD

In 1800 there were 45,000 people living in Ohio. The US government decided that was enough people for Ohio to become a state. The leaders of Ohio created a constitution and a state government with legislative, executive, and judicial branches. These branches write bills, sign bills into law, and apply laws in court cases.

OHIO

QUICK FACTS

Look closely at these facts and symbols of Ohio. How do they help you better understand the state?

Abbreviation: OH
Nickname: The Buckeye State
Motto: With God, all things are possible
Date of statehood: February 19, 1803*
Capital: Columbus
Population: 11,799,448
Area: 44,826 square miles (116,099 sq km)

STATE SYMBOLS

State bird
Northern cardinal

State mammal
White-tailed deer

State native fruit
Pawpaw

State wildflower
White trillium

*Date of statehood later changed to the first meeting of the state legislature on March 1, 1803

PERSPECTIVES

THE 50-STAR FLAG

In 1958 high school student Bob Heft created a 50-star US flag for a school project. At the time, the country had only 48 states. Heft thought Alaska and Hawaii would soon become states, so he sewed together a new design with two extra stars. His teacher gave him a B– because the project didn't seem unique. When Heft protested, his teacher said he would raise the grade if Heft's design became the national flag. Heft asked his Ohio congress member Walter Henry Moeller to take the design to Washington, DC. Two years later, Heft's design was adopted as the new US flag. His teacher changed the grade to an A.

Ohio became the seventeenth state on February 19, 1803. It was the first state carved from the Northwest Territory.

Through the 1800s, more immigrants from Europe arrived in Ohio. They included people from Ireland, Germany, France, and Switzerland. People from other parts of the United States also began moving to Ohio. At first they came because there was land for farming. But even after most of the farmland in Ohio was claimed, opportunities in Ohio continued to grow. Ohio's new residents built factories, paved roads, dug canals, mined coal, and founded colleges. All these developments provided jobs.

Opportunities in Ohio were more promising for white settlers. But the same things were not given to people of other races. Slavery was not allowed in Ohio. However, there were many laws that made life difficult for Black people. They could not attend public schools, vote, serve in the state's militia, or marry white people. They also struggled to find jobs.

In 1861 the American Civil War (1861–1865) began between the Union

PRESIDENTS

Throughout the United States' history, Ohio has had an important role in politics. Eight presidents have come from Ohio. Ulysses S. Grant, Rutherford B. Hayes, James A. Garfield, Benjamin Harrison, William McKinley, William Howard Taft, and Warren G. Harding were all born in Ohio. William Henry Harrison was born in Virginia, but he lived in Ohio when he was elected.

in the North and the Confederacy in the South. Some Ohioans supported the Confederacy. But many supported the Union. Ohio sent many soldiers to fight in the war. This included the famous general Ulysses S. Grant. Grant was in charge of all Union soldiers by the end of the war.

After the Union won the Civil War, Black people in Ohio gained more rights. When most Black Americans could not go to college, Ohio had two colleges that Black people could attend. Oberlin College accepted both Black and white students. Wilberforce University was specifically for Black students. Ohio's citizens also began electing Black men to government positions.

After 1900 Ohio's population of Black people grew. More and more Black people started to leave the South and move north to states including Ohio. They could make more money working in factories in northern cities than they could working on southern farms.

Ulysses S. Grant served as US president shortly after the Civil War, from 1869 to 1877.

Oberlin College is still operating today.

Even though these jobs created better opportunities, Black Americans still faced segregation and discrimination. They could not buy houses in areas where white families lived. Schools in cities were still segregated. These problems continued until the 1970s. Laws finally made discrimination illegal. Cities made solutions to desegregate schools. Today activists in Ohio continue to work to make sure that all people have the same rights and freedoms.

STRAIGHT TO THE SOURCE

After America gained independence from Britain, the British sometimes helped American Indians fight Americans to keep their land. But by the War of 1812, Henry Proctor commanded the British Army in the Americas. He was reluctant to help. Tecumseh told Proctor of his surprise:

> *We are much astonished to see you tying up everything and preparing to run the other way. You always told us to remain here and take care of our lands. It made our hearts glad to hear that was your wish. But now we see you drawing back like a fat animal, running off with its tail between its legs.*
>
> *If you have an idea of going away, leave us the guns and ammunition and you may go and welcome for it. Our lives are in the hands of the Great Spirit. We are determined to defend our lands, and if it is his will, we shall leave our bones upon them.*

Source: "We Shall Remain: Episode Two: Tecumseh's Vision." *PBS American Experience*, n.d., tc.pbs.org. PDF. Accessed 12 July 2021.

WHAT'S THE BIG IDEA?

Consider Tecumseh's words carefully. What is his main point in this speech? What details does he use to support his main point?

CHAPTER THREE

GEOGRAPHY AND CLIMATE

Ohio has five geographic regions. In the northwest corner of Ohio are the Lake Plains. In ancient times, there were huge lakes over this area. When the lakes disappeared, they left behind swampy land covered by forests and floodwater. People drained the swamps in the 1800s, unearthing rich soil. Toward the east is the Glaciated Allegheny Plateau. Ancient glaciers created hills in this area. The land has many forests.

People can enjoy caves at Hocking Hills State Park in southeastern Ohio.

In the southeast corner is the Unglaciated Appalachian Plateau. This mountainous area is rocky. Streams have carved deep valleys into the rocks. Coal, oil, and gas are all found underground here. In a small portion of southeast Ohio is the Bluegrass Region, which has many hills. In the central and western areas of the state are the Till Plains. This area was once covered by glaciers, which left behind huge piles of rock and soil called moraines. The area has gentle hills and soil that is great for farming.

Most of Ohio has a humid continental climate. This means that summers are

LAKE ERIE

Lake Erie is an important part of Ohio's geography. Lake Erie's name comes from the Haudenosaunee word for "long tail." Of the Great Lakes, Lake Erie is the shallowest. This means that it gets warmer than the other Great Lakes in the summer, which makes it a common fishing destination. Lake Erie also has many islands where locals and visitors like to escape for vacation. There are even some playful rumors that a lake monster named Bessie lives in Lake Erie.

Cuyahoga Valley National Park is home to many kinds of birds, including wood ducks.

warm, especially in the south. High temperatures average 90 degrees Fahrenheit (32°C) in July. Winters are cold and snowy, especially in the north. Nights in the north average below 15 degrees Fahrenheit (−9.4°C).

For visitors and locals seeking natural beauty, Ohio has many parks and forests. The Cuyahoga Valley National Park is Ohio's only national park. Visitors here can bike the old Ohio and Erie Canal path, catch a ride on a historic railroad, or hike to waterfalls. Hikers may also enjoy the waterfalls and caves of Hocking Hills State Park, which are famous across the country. Visitors often consider autumn to be the best time to visit Ohio. The leaves of Ohio's forests change into vivid colors at this time.

PERSPECTIVES

PAWPAW

The pawpaw is Ohio's state fruit. The pawpaw tree has big leaves. It produces an oval-shaped fruit. Inside, the fruit has black seeds that are arranged like an animal's paw. Some people say that the pawpaw tastes like a mango but has the texture of a banana. Ohioans have started celebrating the pawpaw, adding it to everything from drinks to desserts. One resident says that pawpaw ice cream is his favorite way to enjoy the unique fruit.

PLANTS AND ANIMALS

Many of Ohio's original trees were cut down when the land was settled, but some forests have been replanted. Now, one-third of Ohio's land is covered by trees. These include oak, ash, maple, walnut, buckeye, basswood, hickory, pawpaw, and beech trees. In the spring and summer, thousands of native wildflowers bloom, including the white trillium, mayapple, and many varieties of violets.

Ohio is a great place to fish. Its lakes and rivers hold fish such as walleyes, bass, trout, muskellunge, and perch. Bird-watchers may spot common birds such as northern cardinals, American robins, red-tailed hawks, mourning doves, and many kinds of woodpeckers and owls. Other common animals include white-tailed deer, foxes, skunks, rabbits, raccoons, and coyotes.

EXPLORE ONLINE

Chapter Three discusses Ohio's geography, including how glaciers shaped its land. The article at the website below has more information about these glaciers. Compare and contrast the information in the article with the facts included in this chapter. What information is the same? What new information did you learn?

GLACIER

abdocorelibrary.com/ohio

CHAPTER FOUR

RESOURCES AND ECONOMY

Throughout Ohio's history, its location has helped its economy grow. Some of the most important resources in Ohio are its rivers and lakes. When Ohio first became a state, there was no easy way to get goods across the Appalachian Mountains to sell in the cities on the East Coast. A canal from the Ohio River to Lake Erie would fix this problem. Construction on the Ohio and Erie Canal began in 1825. This waterway let boats travel from the Ohio River to Lake Erie.

The Ohio and Erie Canal had locks in which the water level could be raised or lowered to help boats travel across the canal.

From there they could travel down another canal to the Hudson River. This river gave boats access to cities including New York City. Farmers could sell their produce more efficiently. The canal and the jobs it created enabled Ohio's population to grow quickly.

Even though the canal is no longer operating, the Ohio River and Lake Erie remain important methods of transportation. Ohio has nine ports along Lake Erie. Ships enter these ports carrying materials such as iron ore and steel products. Factories rely on these shipments to create products including cars, appliances, and machinery. When ships leave Ohio, they take goods with them.

BASED IN OHIO

There are many large companies that manufacture products in Ohio. Goodyear Tire and Rubber makes tires for vehicles. Sherwin-Williams makes paint for homes. J. M. Smucker is the company that produces Jif peanut butter and Smucker's jelly. Procter & Gamble is based in Ohio too. It makes Tide detergent, Charmin toilet paper, Dawn dish soap, and Crest toothpaste.

Ohio's waters, including Lake Erie, are important for shipping goods.

They might carry grain to other countries or coal to other states to produce electricity.

MANUFACTURING AND FARMING

Ohio has many natural resources that are needed to make goods in factories. Ohio's mines produce coal, iron ore, natural gas, a rock salt called halite, and limestone. These resources are either shipped to other states or turned into goods in Ohio's factories. Factories in the state produce chemicals, metal products, processed foods, and automobiles and motor parts.

As Ohio industrialized during the 1800s, the state struggled with pollution. Many factories dumped their waste into the rivers. The waters became very polluted.

One river near Cleveland, the Cuyahoga River, was so full of oil that it caught on fire multiple times. The most famous time was in 1969. The fire lasted for at least 20 minutes and damaged a bridge and other property. This wasn't the biggest or most damaging fire on the Cuyahoga, but the story was published in a national magazine. People paid attention. This fire became a symbol of pollution. Congress established

PERSPECTIVES

CLEANER WATERS

Though Ohio's lakes and rivers are cleaner than they were 50 years ago, pollution is still significant. Fertilizers from farm fields wash into rivers and cause thick, toxic algae to form. This makes swimming in the water or drinking it dangerous. Chemicals from mining and manufacturing are also still present in the water. It's considered risky to eat fish caught from the Ohio River. Timothy Buckley, a professor in environmental health sciences, worried that citizens may not realize the importance of keeping the waters clean. He said, "People may miss the connection between protection of natural resources and their own health." But a growing number of Ohioans are advocating for cleaner water.

the Environmental Protection Agency partly in reaction to this fire.

Farming is the biggest industry in Ohio. More than half of Ohio's land is used for farming. Farmers in Ohio grow many crops. Soybeans and corn are the most popular. Farmers also grow grains to feed livestock. Other crops include a variety of fruits and vegetables. Growers in Ohio also produce many flowers, trees, and other plants sold in nurseries and greenhouses. Some farmers raise livestock such as chickens, turkeys, sheep, pigs, and cattle.

FURTHER EVIDENCE

Chapter Four discusses Ohio's resources and economy. Identify one of the author's main points in this chapter. What evidence does the author provide to support this point? The article at the website below also discusses the topic. Find a quote at the website that supports the author's main point. Does it offer a new piece of evidence?

OHIO

abdocorelibrary.com/ohio

OHIO
MARQUETTE

PEOPLE AND PLACES

The people of Ohio are known as Ohioans. Several famous people have come from Ohio. They include director Steven Spielberg, sharpshooter Annie Oakley, professional basketball player LeBron James, and astronaut Neil Armstrong.

In Ohio, white people who are not Hispanic or Latino make up 78.4 percent of the population. The next largest group is Black people at 13.1 percent. Hispanic and Latino people make up 4 percent, and 2.5 percent

Jesse Owens, *left*, was a famous track-and-field athlete from Ohio.

PERSPECTIVES

JESSE OWENS

Jesse Owens, a record-setting Black track-and-field athlete, was from Cleveland. While Owens was attending the Ohio State University in 1935, he matched or broke multiple world records in track and field. Owens is most famous for his performance at the 1936 Olympic Games in Berlin, Germany. Owens won four gold medals.

are Asian. These last two groups are growing faster than any other population in Ohio. American Indians make up 0.3 percent. There are no federally recognized tribes in the state.

Museums and attractions across the state celebrate Ohio's people and history. At the National Underground Railroad Freedom Center in Cincinnati, guests can learn about enslaved people's journeys to freedom. Those journeys often began as they crossed the Ohio River into Ohio. The Ohio History Center in Columbus has artifacts from Ohio's history. Visitors see ancient mastodon bones, American Indian artifacts, and restored Civil War flags. More museums across the state feature exhibits on automobiles, submarines, the US Air Force, aviation, and the lives of Ohioan presidents.

ART AND SCIENCE

Ohio is also a center for the arts and science. Many famous writers hail from Ohio. Paul Laurence Dunbar was one of the first famous Black poets in the late 1800s and early 1900s. Toni Morrison and Rita Dove, two award-winning poets from Ohio, have written about Black women's experiences.

FOOD IN COLUMBUS

Columbus is often considered a test city for restaurants and businesses trying new products. Residents in Columbus have been able to try new Starbucks drinks and new Wendy's sandwiches before anyone else in the country. One reason is Ohio's population. The percentages of people from different races in Columbus are close to the country's average. This makes it easier for companies to predict how a product will perform nationally. Columbus also has many young people at its universities who might be interested in trying new things.

The Rock and Roll Hall of Fame opened its building and museum in Cleveland in 1995.

Ohio has plenty of art museums. Museums in Akron, Dayton, Toledo, Cleveland, and Cincinnati have reputations across the country for being excellent places to study both ancient and modern works of art. Ohio's music scene is also legendary. Orchestras in Cleveland, Toledo, Dayton, and Cincinnati are known as some of the best in the nation. Cleveland is home to the Rock and Roll Hall of Fame. Ohio is the only state to have an official rock song. "Hang On Sloopy" by the Ohio band the McCoys is often played at sporting events.

Many Ohio inventors helped develop forms of transportation. Some of Granville Woods's inventions helped improve railroads. Ohioan John Lambert invented America's first usable gasoline automobile, and Charles Kettering later created the first self-starting electric car motor. The Wright brothers, also from Ohio, made history when they made a powered, sustained, and controlled airplane flight.

OHIO'S SPORTS

People in Ohio are very passionate about sports. Ohio has professional football, basketball, hockey, and baseball teams. Ohio is especially passionate about football. It was home to the United States' very first professional football league, the American Professional Football Association, in 1920. The Pro Football Hall of Fame in Canton celebrates the accomplishments of

Fans enjoy cheering on their team and sometimes meeting their favorite players at the Buckeyes' stadium.

National Football League players. And today Saturdays often find fans flocking to the football stadium at the Ohio State University to cheer on the Buckeyes.

Ohio is rich in activities and history. Visitors and residents alike can enjoy the arts, science, and history in the state. From city to countryside, Ohio offers many adventures.

STRAIGHT TO THE SOURCE

In the 1985 resolution to make "Hang On Sloopy" Ohio's state rock song, the state congress used casual and humorous language:

> *WHEREAS, "Hang On Sloopy" is of particular relevance to members of the Baby Boom Generation, who were once dismissed as a bunch of long-haired, crazy kids, but who now are old enough and vote in sufficient numbers to be taken quite seriously; and*
>
> *WHEREAS, Adoption of this resolution will not take too long, cost the state anything, or affect the quality of life in this state to any appreciable degree, and if we in the legislature just go ahead and pass [it], we can get on with more important stuff.*

Source: "Ohio's State Rock Song." *Ohio History Central*, n.d., ohiohistorycentral.org. Accessed 13 July 2021.

CONSIDER YOUR AUDIENCE

Read this passage carefully. Consider how you would adapt it for a different audience, such as your younger friends. Write a blog post conveying this same information to the new audience. Write it so that it can be understood by them. How does your new approach differ from the original text, and why?

IMPORTANT DATES

9500 BCE
Early people are living in present-day Ohio.

1670s
The first Europeans arrive in Ohio.

1763
The French and Indian War ends, giving control of Ohio's lands to the British.

1783
American forces win the Revolutionary War. Present-day Ohio becomes part of the United States of America.

1803
Ohio becomes the seventeenth state on February 19.

1861
The American Civil War begins. Ohio sends many troops to fight for the Union.

1969
Oil in the Cuyahoga River catches on fire and burns for at least 20 minutes. This fire and others prompt people to work to clean up the river.

1985
"Hang On Sloopy" becomes Ohio's state rock song.

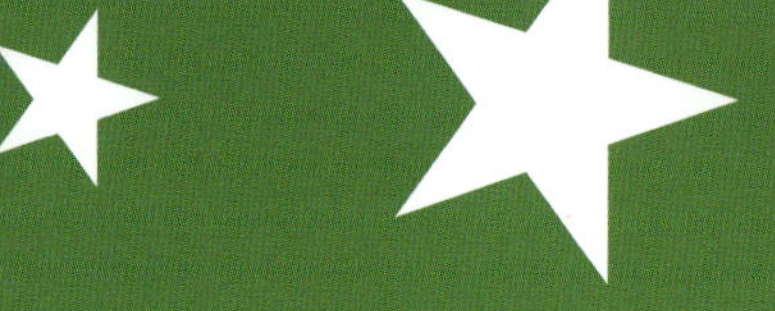

STOP AND THINK

Tell the Tale

Chapter One describes the experience of riding the Millennium Force roller coaster at Cedar Point. Imagine you are riding that roller coaster. How do you feel? What do you see? Explain your experience in 200 words.

Say What?

Studying a state's history and economy can mean learning a lot of new vocabulary. Find five words in this book you've never heard before. Use a dictionary to find out what they mean. Then write the meanings in your own words and use each word in a new sentence.

Why Do I Care?

Chapter Four discusses pollution in Ohio. You may not live in a place with a lot of pollution, but that doesn't mean you can't think about how pollution affects you. Have you visited a place with pollution? How might pollution in some of Ohio's lakes and rivers affect people who don't live near them? Why should people help clean up pollution?

Another View

This book talks about the War of 1812. As you know, every source is different. Ask a librarian or another adult to help you find another source about this event. Write a short essay comparing and contrasting the new source's point of view with that of this book's author. What is the point of view of each author? How are they similar and why? How are they different and why?

GLOSSARY

canal
a long, human-made ditch that allows water to flow from one area to another

discrimination
when people treat others differently based on certain factors such as appearance

economy
a place's system of goods, services, money, and jobs

glacier
a large body of ice that moves across land

mastodon
an extinct mammal with tusks and a trunk, similar to an elephant

militia
a group of citizens who form a military force

pelt
an animal's skin and fur

petroglyph
a prehistoric rock carving

segregation
the separation of groups of people based on race, class, or ethnicity

sustained
ongoing for a period of time without weakening or stopping

ONLINE RESOURCES

To learn more about Ohio, visit our free resource websites below.

Visit **abdocorelibrary.com** or scan this QR code for free Common Core resources for teachers and students, including vetted activities, multimedia, and booklinks, for deeper subject comprehension.

Visit **abdobooklinks.com** or scan this QR code for free additional online weblinks for further learning. These links are routinely monitored and updated to provide the most current information available.

LEARN MORE

Dunphy, Maureen. *All about the Great Lakes*. Blue River, 2019.

O'Brien, Cynthia. *Encyclopedia of American Indian History and Culture*. National Geographic, 2019.

INDEX

About the Author

Anna Saxton is an author and educator. Trained as a teacher, she began her career teaching middle school English. She now specializes in writing books and curricula for students. Her favorite things include good books, strong tea, and the great outdoors.